LIFE'S TREASURE BOOK

D0095501

On Friendship

H. JACKSON BROWN, JR.

Published in Nashville, Tennessee, by Rutledge Hill Press, a Thomas Nelson Company, P.O. Box 141000, Nashville, Tennessee 37214.

Book design by Karen Phillips and Nikita Pristouris

ISBN: 1-55853-802-X

Printed in the United States of America

1 2 3 4 5 6 7 8 9—04 03 02 01 00

Introduction

What is more welcome than the sound of a friend's voice, the sight of her smiling face, the warmth of an embrace? It is one of life's finest blessings to have a friend with whom we can safely discuss our fears and enthusiastically share our dreams—someone who accepts us totally as we are in spite of our shortcomings.

A true friend encourages us, comforts us, supports us like a big easy chair, offering us a safe refuge from the world. A true friend stands at our side during the best and the worst of times. A true friend listens when we need to talk through a problem. A true friend answers the phone at midnight and does not resent the call. A true friend will defend us to the world.

We speak of "friends and acquaintances" because we know the difference. Acquaintances we meet, enjoy, and can easily leave behind; but friendship grows deep roots. Even when we are separated by time and distance, friendship continues to grow and mature. We've all had the experience of meeting an old friend after many years and discovering that we are able to renew our relationship as if the separation had only been a few minutes.

A Nigerian proverb advises, "Hold a true friend with both hands." True and faithful friends are indeed a treasure, touching our hearts and strengthening our spirit with their words, their touch, and sometimes by just their silent presence.

Become the

world's most

thoughtful friend.

Offer to pay for parking
and tolls when you are the
passenger in a friend's car.

Friendships are fragile things
and require as much care
in handling as any other fragile
thing and precious thing.

—RANDOLPH S. BOURNE

Friendship improves happiness
and abates misery by doubling
our joy and dividing our grief.

—JOSEPH ADDISON

*I*f you know a friend
has had a bad day,
take her out for coffee
or maybe dinner.

$\mathscr{I}$'ve learned that…

… an act of love, no matter how great or small, is always appreciated.

—AGE 22

… the importance of fame, fortune, and all other things pales in comparison to the importance of positive personal relationships.

—AGE 50

$\mathcal{B}$e the first to say, "Hello."

$\sim$

$\mathcal{B}$e forgiving of yourself
and others.

$\sim$

$\mathcal{T}$reat everyone you meet as
you want to be treated.

Except in cases of necessity,
which are rare,
leave your friend to learn
unpleasant things from
his enemies; they are ready
enough to tell him.

—OLIVER WENDELL HOLMES

$\mathcal{D}$on't forget a person's greatest emotional need is to feel appreciated.

Instead of loving your enemies, treat your friends a little better.

—EDGAR WATSON HOWE

*K*eep secrets.

*C*ompliment three people
every day.

*R*emember other
people's birthdays.

Blessed are they who have the
gift of making friends for it is
one of God's best gifts.
It involves many things,
but above all the power of
going out of one's self
and appreciating whatever is
noble and loving in another.

—THOMAS HUGHES

$\mathcal{I}$'ve learned that…

. . . the friend you just met can be a truer friend than the one you've known all your life.

—AGE 23

. . . it's best to ask for what you need from your friends and not assume that *somehow* they'll just know.

—AGE 34

My friends are my estate.

—Emily Dickinson

*R*eturn borrowed vehicles
with the gas tank full.

$\mathcal{T}$hink twice before
burdening a friend
with a secret.

$\mathcal{N}$ever tell friends
that they look
tired or depressed.

I've learned that…

. . . my best friends are usually the ones who get me in trouble.

—AGE 11

. . . a good relationship between me and my family, my friends, and my business associates can be boiled down to one word: *respect.*

—AGE 56

One friend in a lifetime is
much; two are many;
three are hardly possible.

—HENRY BROOKS ADAMS

To find a friend one
must close one eye.
To keep him . . . two.

—NORMAN DOUGLAS

*C*ut out complimentary newspaper articles about your friends and mail the articles to them with notes of congratulations.

Friendship is Love

without his wings!

—LORD BYRON

$\mathscr{I}$'ve learned that...

. . . a good friend is better
than a therapist.

—AGE 19

. . . when you and your best
friend move away from each
other to attend different
colleges, you start saying
"love ya" at the end of
your phone conversations.

—AGE 18

Be courteous to all,
but intimate with few,
and let those few be well tried
before you give them your
confidence. True friendship is a
plant of slow growth and must
undergo and withstand the shocks
of adversity before it is entitled
to the appellation.

—GEORGE WASHINGTON

$\mathcal{N}$ever underestimate the power of words to heal and reconcile relationships.

Never explain—your friends do not need it and your enemies will not believe it anyhow.

—ELBERT HUBBARD

$\mathcal{I}$'ve learned that…

…moving away from my closest friends was much, much harder to do than I ever thought it would be.

—AGE 26

…there is a great thrill in making pickles and jellies with the same friend I used to make mud pies with.

—AGE 60

If a man does not make new
acquaintance as he advances
through life, he will soon find
himself left alone. A man,
Sir, should keep his friendship
in constant repair.

—Samuel Johnson

$\mathcal{S}$urprise a new neighbor
with one of your favorite
homemade dishes—
and include the recipe.

A father's a treasure;
a brother's a comfort;
a friend is both.

—BENJAMIN FRANKLIN

Years and years
of happiness only make
us realize how lucky we
are to have friends that
have shared and made that
happiness a reality.

—ROBERT E. FREDERICK

$\mathcal{I}$'ve learned that...

. . . when I surprise an old friend with a phone call, it will seem like just yesterday that we last spoke.

—AGE 38

. . . no matter how much a friend promises not to tell anyone else, she always does.

—AGE 16

True friendship comes
when silence between
two people is comfortable.

—DAVE TYSON GENTRY

When meeting someone
for the first time,
resist asking what they
do for a living.
Enjoy their company
without attaching any labels.

$\mathcal{V}$isit friends when they
are in the hospital.
You only need to stay
for a few minutes.

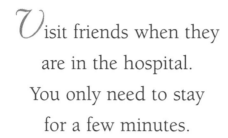

You can always tell a true friend:
when you make a fool of
yourself he doesn't think you've
done a permanent job.

—LAWRENCE J. PETER

$\mathcal{I}$'ve learned that…

. . . being too quick to judge someone can deprive you of a great encounter and the possibility of a wonderful long-term relationship.

—AGE 40

. . . you should never underestimate the power of a hug from a friend.

—AGE 25

*Old friends are
the best friends.*

It is great to have friends
when one is young,
but indeed it is still more
so when you are getting old.
When we are young,
friends are, like everything
else, a matter of course.
In the old days we know what
it means to have them.

—EDVARD GRIEG

$\mathcal{I}$'ve learned that...

. . . sisters can be like
best friends and best friends
can be like sisters.

—AGE 34

. . . nothing beats a hot
summer night, a car full
of friends, the windows
down, music playing, and
whistling at boys!

—AGE 18

Be more prompt
to go to a friend
in adversity than
in prosperity.

—CHILO

Each friend represents
a world in us, a world
possibly not born until
they arrive, and it is
only by this meeting
that a new world is born.

—ANAÏS NIN

$\mathcal{I}$'ve learned that...

... meeting interesting people depends less on where you go than on who you are.

—AGE 51

... a smile, a "How are you?" and a warm, close, caring hug always give love, faith, and hope.

—AGE 54

*T*ake allowances
for your friends'
imperfections as readily
as you do for your own.

A new friend
doubles your net worth.

Give me a few friends
who will love me
for what I am,
or am not, and keep
ever burning before
my wandering steps the
kindly light of hope.

—Anonymous

$\mathcal{I}$'ve learned that...

. . . you can never be too good a listener when a friend is in need.

—AGE 13

. . . when writing letters to friends, if I put a quoted verse or poem on the outside of the envelope, it's like sending a warm hug through the mail.

—AGE 50

A true friend is the greatest
of all blessings, and that
which we take the least care
of all to acquire.

—François de La Rochefoucauld

To the query, "What is a friend?"
his reply was, "A single soul
dwelling in two bodies."

—Aristotle

All men have their
frailties; and whoever
looks for a friend without
imperfections will never
find what he seeks.
We love ourselves
notwithstanding our faults,
and we ought to love our
friends in like manner.

—CYRUS

*T*urn enemies into
friends by doing
something nice for them.

~~

*A*sk for double prints when
you have film processed.
Send the extras to your
friends in the photos.

$\mathcal{I}$'ve learned that…

. . . when I wave to people in the country, they stop what they are doing and wave back.

—AGE 24

. . . you never realize how many wonderful friends you have until your car breaks down.

—AGE 22

I've often wished that I had clear,

For life, six hundred pounds a year,

A handsome house to lodge a friend,

A river at my garden's end,

A terrace walk, and half a rood

Of land, set out to plant a wood.

—JONATHAN SWIFT

$\mathcal{A}$ friend is someone you can call at three in the morning and say, "I'm in a jail in Tijuana." And he says, "Don't worry, I'm on my way."

Hold a true friend with both hands.

—NIGERIAN PROVERB

I've learned that…

… you can never have too many friends.

—AGE 16

… warmth, kindness, and friendship are the most yearned for commodities in the world. The person who can provide them will never be lonely.

—AGE 79

The most I can do for
my friend is simply to be
his friend. I have no wealth
to bestow on him. If he
knows that I am happy in
loving him, he will want
no other reward. Is not
friendship divine in this?

—HENRY DAVID THOREAU

*I*ntroduce yourself to
your neighbors as soon
as you move into
a new neighborhood.

~

*W*hen a friend becomes ill,
remember that hope and
positive thinking are
strong medicines.

$\mathscr{I}$'ve learned that…

. . . the greatest test of friendship is to take a vacation
together and still like each
other when you return.

—AGE 59

. . . my best friend and I can
do anything or nothing and
have the best time.

—AGE 18

*Never injure
a friend,
even in jest.*

—Cicero

$\mathcal{A}$ friend is someone
who knows you and
loves you for what you were
and who you are,
and who also shares
your hopes and dreams for
who you can become.

The better part of
one's life consists
of his friendships.

—ABRAHAM LINCOLN

$\mathcal{I}$'ve learned that…

. . . I would rather have a best friend than a boyfriend, except maybe on a Friday night.

—AGE 20

. . . a good friend is the one who tells you how you really look in your jeans.

—AGE 25

I awoke this morning with
devout thanksgiving for my
friends, the old and the new.

—RALPH WALDO EMERSON

Love is only chatter,
Friends are all that matter.

—GELETT BURGESS

Surprise an old friend
with a phone call.

Don't take good friends,
good health, or a good
marriage for granted.

Don't let a little dispute
injure a great friendship.

$\mathcal{I}$'ve learned that…

… I need to let my friends comfort me and hold me up, to let them know I need support, that I'm not always as strong as I look or act.

—AGE 49

… having a young friend when you are old is a special joy.

—AGE 83

From quiet houses and first
    beginning,
Out to the undiscovered ends,
There's nothing worth the
    wear of winning,
But laughter and the love of
    friends.

—HILAIRE BELLOC

$\mathcal{I}$'ve learned that...

...true friendship continues to grow, even over the longest distance.

—AGE 19

...in this world, you don't need a multitude of friends. All you really need is one who will stand by you through thick and thin.

—AGE 34

Do not keep the alabaster boxes
of your love and
tenderness sealed up until
your friends are dead.
Fill their lives with sweetness.
Speak approving, cheering words
while their ears can
hear them and while their hearts
can be thrilled by them.

—HENRY WARD BEECHER

A friend is a present
you give to yourself.

—Robert Louis Stevenson

$\mathcal{B}$e mindful that happiness
is not based on possessions,
power, or prestige, but on
relationships with people
you love and respect.

$\mathcal{I}$'ve learned that…

. . . if you're not willing to
move mountains for your
friends, they won't be willing
to move them for you.

—AGE 18

. . . one of the best things
I can give a hurting friend is
my presence, not my words.

—AGE 38

*B*y friendship you mean
the greatest love, the greatest
usefulness, the most noble
sufferings, the severest truth,
 the heartiest counsel,
and the greatest union
of minds of which brave men
and women are capable.

—Jeremy Taylor

*R*ekindle an old
friendship.

*O*ffer to leave the tip
when a friend invites
you out to eat.

*C*all before dropping in
on a friend.

Life has no blessing like
a prudent friend.

—EURIPIDES

It is one of the blessings
of old friends that you
can afford to be
stupid with them.

—RALPH WALDO EMERSON

$\mathcal{L}$ook for opportunities
to make people
feel important.

$\mathcal{W}$hen friends offer
to help, let them.

When you hear
a kind word
spoken about
a friend,
tell him so.

I've learned that…

… the best remedy for a bad day is two cups of hot chocolate with marshmallows, a plate of chocolate-chip cookies warm from the oven, and a friend.

—AGE 31

… there are good neighbors wherever you live.

—AGE 30

Two persons cannot long be friends if they cannot forgive each other's little failings.

—Jean de la Bruyère

A faithful friend is
the medicine of life.

—ECCLESIASTES 6:6

A friend is a person with whom
I may be sincere. Before him
I may think aloud.

—RALPH WALDO EMERSON

$\mathcal{A}$sk someone you'd like to know better to list five people he would most like to meet. It will tell you a lot about him.

$\mathcal{B}$e open and accessible.
The next person you meet
could become your best friend.

There is nothing so great that
I fear to do it for my friend;
nothing so small that
I will disdain to do it for him.

—SIR PHILIP SIDNEY

$\mathcal{I}$'ve learned that...

. . . when you're too
busy for your friends,
you're too busy.

—AGE 48

. . . no matter how good
a friend someone is,
they're going to hurt
you every once in a while
and you must forgive them
for that.

—AGE 18

A true friend is the
gift of God.

—ROBERT SOUTH

Friendship has the skill and
observation of the best
physician, the diligence and
vigilance of the best nurse,
and the patience and
tenderness of the best mother.

—EDWARD CLARENDON

With every friend I love who has been taken into the brown bosom of earth, a part of me has been buried there; but their contributions to my being of happiness, strength, and understanding remain to sustain me in an altered world.

—HELEN KELLER

The only way to have a
friend is to be one.

—RALPH WALDO EMERSON

*R*emember that the shortest
way to get anywhere is to have a
friend traveling with you.

$\mathscr{I}$'ve learned that…

. . . it makes me happy to see the answering machine light flashing when I get home.

—AGE 18

. . . people love to get letters from friends no matter what the subject is or the length of the letters.

—AGE 22

Fortify yourself with a flock
of friends! You can select them
at random, write to one,
dine with one, visit one,
or take your problems to one.
There is always at least one
who will understand, inspire,
and give you the lift you
need at the time.

—GEORGE MATTHEW ADAMS

The loss of a friend
is like that of a limb;
time may heal the anguish
of the wound, but the
loss cannot be repaired.

—Robert Southey

$\mathcal{I}$'ve learned that…

. . . you shouldn't judge people too quickly. Sometimes they have a good reason for the way they act.

—AGE 20

. . . people will remember you as being a great conversationalist if you mostly listen.

—AGE 49

$\mathcal{R}$emember that no time is
ever wasted that makes
two people better friends.

Love and friendship are the
discoveries of ourselves in
others, and our delight in
the recognition.

—ALEXANDER SMITH

Friendship is the
only cement that
will ever hold the
world together.

—WOODROW WILSON

$\mathcal{M}$eet regularly with
friends who hold vastly
different views than you.

$\mathcal{D}$on't forget that a
couple of words of praise
or encouragement can
make someone's day.

I've learned that...

. . . the definition of a best
friend is someone who listens
to me and knows that I will
always return the favor.

—Age 23

. . . it's not the big things
that you do for your friends
that they remember; it's the
little things.

—Age 62

In poverty and other
misfortunes of life,
true friends are a sure refuge.
The young, they keep out of
mischief; to the old,
they are a comfort and aid
in their weakness; and to those
in the prime of life,
they incite to noble deeds.

—ARISTOTLE

$\mathcal{I}$'ve learned that…

… whatever your life lacks, such as parents, sisters, or brothers, God will give you a substitute and it usually takes the form of a wonderful friend.

—AGE 39

… it's never too late to show your friends you appreciate them.

—AGE 23

When a friend is in need,
help him without his
having to ask.

~~

Call three friends on
Thanksgiving and tell them
how thankful you are for
their friendship.

Go oft to the house of
thy friend, for weeds choke
the unused path.

—Ralph Waldo Emerson

When a friend gets a new car, tell him how terrific it looks and ask to go for a ride.

$\mathcal{I}$'ve learned that…

. . . when I want advice,
I call my best friend. When
I want sympathy, I call
my boyfriend.

—AGE 48

. . . no matter how serious
your life requires you to be,
everyone needs a friend to
act goofy with.

—AGE 21

When someone you know is down and out, anonymously mail him or her a twenty-dollar bill.

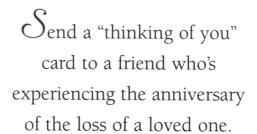

Send a "thinking of you" card to a friend who's experiencing the anniversary of the loss of a loved one.

When someone
hugs you, let them be
the first to let go.

True friendship is like
sound health, the value
of it is seldom known
until it be lost.

—CHARLES CALEB COLTON

*W*hen you see someone
sitting alone on a bench,
make it a point to
speak to them.

Think where man's glory
most begins and ends,
And say my glory was
I had such friends.

—W. B. Yeats

A friend may well
be reckoned the
masterpiece of Nature.

—Ralph Waldo Emerson